Maxamed Xaashi Dhamac 'Gaarriye'

Ask the Thunder
Onkodka Warayso

Translated from Somali by
W.N. Herbert and Martin Orwin

poetry
translation
centre

First published in 2020
by the Poetry Translation Centre Ltd
The Albany, Douglas Way, London, SE8 4AG

www.poetrytranslation.org

Poems © Maxamed Xaashi Dhamac 'Gaarriye' 2012
English Translations ©W.N. Herbert and Martin Orwin 2020
Introduction © Martin Orwin 2020
Afterword © Clare Pollard 2019

Some of these poems first appeared in the chapbook *Poems* (Enitharmon Press; 2008).

ISBN: 978-1-9161141-1-1

A catalogue record for this book is available from the British Library

Typeset in Minion by Poetry Translation Centre Ltd

Series Editor: Edward Doegar
Cover Design: Kit Humphrey
Printed in the UK by T.J. International

The PTC is supported using public funding by
Arts Council England

Contents

Introduction	7
Self-misunderstood *(1972)*	15
Seer *(1984)*	25
Death of a Princess *(1981)*	33
Arrogance *(1973)*	45
Watergate *(1977)*	51
Afterword	57
About the contributors	64
About the series	66

Introduction

The 1970s were a pivotal time for Somali literature for a number of reasons. Poets were using forms in innovative ways; the first official script for Somali was introduced in 1972; cassette tapes were increasingly being used to disseminate what was, and still is to a large extent, oral, and certainly heard, poetry; musical accompaniment was moving in new directions; written prose fiction was being published and all of this was set against the political background of the military regime which had taken power by coup in 1969 following just over nine years of independence. Poets played a very important role in commenting on these times and one of the most significant of these was Maxamed Xaashi Dhamac 'Gaarriye'.

Gaarriye was born in Hargeysa in 1949 into a poor family background and was brought up first by an aunt Ruun Dhamac and then, following her death, by a friend of hers Biliso, who features in the poem 'Uurkubbaale' ('Seer'). He attended Biyo Dhacay School in Hargeysa and the secondary school in Shiikh before going on to Lafoole College in Afgooye near Mogadishu from where, in 1974, he graduated in biology.

His passion for poetry had begun at an early age and a particular favourite was Cabdullaahi Suldaan Maxamed 'Timocadde' for whom Gaarriye wrote a powerful elegy when he died in 1973. Timocadde's important political poems in the run-up to independence, his sense of justice and his technique in making poems were influential on Gaarriye. It was not only Somali poetry however; he studied Arabic poetry at school which was an influence on his development as a poet and a scholar and I recall him mentioning both Abū al-Qāsim al-Shābbī and Nizār Qabbānī as being particular influences later in life. Whilst a student at Lafoole he was part of a group of young poets and playwrights who, in the immediate aftermath of the coup produced influential work, a highlight of which was the play Aqoon iyo Afgarad (Knowledge and Understanding) which they wrote together. The others in the group were Saciid Saalax Axmed and Muuse Cabdi Cilmi along with Maxamed Ibraahim Warsame 'Hadraawi' who was working as a teacher in Mogadishu at the time.

These poets, along with others living both in Somalia and Djibouti (the latter only gaining independence in 1977) were also central to the 'Siinley' (The One Alliterating in 'S') a poetry chain which addressed issues facing the Somali Horn at the time and, given the hostility of the regime to criticism, used metaphor and imagery to create imaginative political allegories which became very popular, and some of which are still well known today.

Following graduation, Gaarriye worked as a secondary school teacher for a couple of years before returning to Lafoole to teach Somali literature and becoming the head of the department shortly thereafter. He continued to write poems—and he did use writing to make his poems, he didn't memorize them—in which he addressed a variety of themes. He wrote two ars poetica poems, one of which is translated in this volume. In this he stresses not only the importance of craft and of making a poem that speaks deeply to the listener, but also the responsibilities of poets to use their skills wisely and for the good. This sense of responsibility as a poet in Somali society was couched in a sense of curiosity about the world and the place of humanity within it. In the fascinating poem 'Garaad-daran' ('Self-misunderstood') he questions himself as a human being within the span of history. In trying to understand himself, his poem speaks to us as he leads us to try to make sense of our own being and behaviour.

Addressing injustice was at the heart of much of his work. Whether in the Horn of Africa or further afield, he expressed himself in 'the best words for the best thoughts'

('Uurkubbaale'). His language is rich but does not rely too much on the traditional imagery of the nomadic background, which continued to be commonly used at the time, thus making them more accessible to a wider audience particularly in the growing urban areas as well as in the countryside. We see this in 'Geeridii Ina Boqor' ('Death of a Princess'). In this more narrative poem he draws on images which reference the countryside, but in Saudi Arabia, and in a way that sets the scene metaphorically for the main topic. 'Wootargayt' ('Watergate') nods occasionally to traditionally used imagery but the language here is much more direct, whilst still vivid. This reflects the straightforward address to President Carter and to the United States after that country initially vetoed Angola's joining the United Nations.

'Wootargayt' is in the long-line gabay form which Gaarriye did not use often, preferring shorter-line forms. In his use of metre he could be innovative and used children's song metrical patterns for some poems which were nevertheless of a serious nature. This novel use of metrical patterning reflects his interest in metre which had begun in school when he had studied it in Arabic poetry. He subsequently developed ideas regarding metre in Somali poetry and in 1976 was the first to publish on this topic in a series of seminal articles in the national newspaper of the time, Xiddigta Oktoobar (October Star), which set out a clear and insightful analysis of how the metrical system works.

His engagement in political commentary through poetry reached a height when he wrote a poem at the end of 1979 alliterating in 'd' about the political situation in Somalia at the time and the matter of clannism. This was responded to first by Hadraawi and then by a long series of poems by all the major figures of the time resulting in a highly significant chain of poems, the 'Deelley' (The One Alliterating in 'D') which is still remembered today. Shortly afterwards, in 1982, he joined one of the opposition groups, the Somali National

Movement, based at the time in Ethiopia and continued to be an influential voice through his poetry during the 1980s. After the ousting of the regime of Maxamed Siyaad Barre in 1991 Gaarriye returned to Hargeysa. In the same year, Somaliland declared itself a separate state but conflict continued in parts of that territory for a few years and Gaarriye once again spoke powerfully against this in such poems as the geeraar of 1992 'Ergo' ('Delegate / Arbitrator').

He lived for the rest of his life in Hargeysa and taught Somali literature and some biology at the University of Amoud and the University of Hargeysa. His lectures on literature were very popular and are still fondly remembered by his former students some of whom he helped over and above his duties as teacher. He died in 2012 after serious illness which became apparent in Norway where he had gone to teach Somali language and literature for a few weeks to Somali diaspora teachers in Scandinavia at Hedmark University College in Hamar. His wonderful poems mean that his memory lives on as does his influence on poetry, its role and its study.

Martin Orwin

Poems

Garaad-daran

Garaad-daran naftaydaay!
Geeri iyo nololeey!
Guluf lagu negaadaay!
Gabno laga dhergaayeey!
Gabbal dumay habeenoo
Hadh gadiidan yahayeey!
Lammaan aan is-geyinoo
Guri qudh ah u hooydaay!

Googgaada xaajada
Gaaxdeedu waxay tahay,
Maan garan xogtaadee,
Maxaad uga gol leedahay?

Ma wax gaar ah baad too
Goonidiisa jira oo
Garab aan u baahnayn?
Mise gobol dad-weynaha
Ka go'aynnin baad tahay?

Maadigaa ah Gaarriye?
Mise laba gudboonoo
Is-geleynin baad tiin?
Gurrac-loo-abuuryeey,
Bal geddaada ii sheeg.

Garaad-daran naftaydaay!
Gurey iyo cadceedaha

Self-misunderstood

I can't understand you, curious self,
nor grasp how you're both life and death,
grabbed land and peaceful settlement,
grudging milker that makes me full,
sun set at evening whilst casting
noon's shortest shadow: how can you be
two who can't marry
yet share the same house?

How can I set this riddle and
give away its answer if
I fail to understand your secret
or even what you mean by it?

Are you something separate,
a stand-alone that leans
upon no man's shoulder,
or such a part of the people
that you can't be parted from them?

And are you that which is Gaarriye
or two opposing halves
he cannot fit together?
I call you, crooked creation:
bear witness to your character.

I can't get to grips with you, gregarious self
are you the same age as Gurey

Isku gedo miyaad tiin?
Gacal miyaad wadaagtaan?

Bal Giriig warkiisiyo
Guutadii Fircoon iyo
Waxa boqor la gawracay,
Ama aad gariir iyo
Guri ba'ay u taagnayd,
Googoos u mariyoo;

Giddi waaxyahaygiyo
U galaydh xubnaha oo;
Midba gees u taagoo
Ka gur sheekadoodoo;
Malaayiin gu' oo tegey
Ku dheh gebaggebeeyoo;
Geeddigoodi dheeraa
Mid kastaa guduudiga,
Halkay galabba joogtiyo
Goorteey kulmeenee
Gaarriye sameeyeen,
Godolkeeda ii mari.

Garaad-daran naftaydaay!
Sida gacanka Waaheen
Hadba gaaf-wareegaay!
Arrin aad gorfeysiyo
Waxaad shalay u guuxdaad,
Maantana ka giigtaa
Gol-daloolo yeeshee;

and his fellow constellations?
Are you all kin?

And what about the history of the Greeks,
the Pharaoh's army and
the goring of kings,
what about the groans of war,
the dynasties you saw destroyed?
Bear witness to it all.

My limbs and all their molecules,
call them to the stand:
line them up in ranks,
collect their statements;
those million monsoons that marched past,
tell them to complete
the tale of that trek
which each one took, the night-walking
and the assignations,
where they were each afternoon
when they made Gaarriye:
make their stories flow like milk.

I can't seem to fix you, quarrelsome self,
you're like that riverbed, Waaheen,
shifting between long drought, brief spate –
that business you concluded yesterday,
signed, sealed and celebrated,
today you snatch it back
and poke it full of holes.

Miyaad dhalan-geddoontoo
Dib bay kuu gardaadsheen?
Ma runtaa gaboowdoo
Geedkeedu waareyn?
Guul-darradu dhankay tahay?

Guud ahaan waxaad tahay
Dadku kugu go'doonyoo
Isla waa go'aanoo,
Mid baad geesi adagoo
Gabbanayn la tahayoo;
Maan-gaab lumaayiyo
Mid baa ceel ganuuniyo
Kuu haysta gocoroo;
Mid baa kugu goblama oo
Gurxankiisu damihayn
Haddii saxar ku gaadhoo;
Gaadaa wax boobiyo
Mid baad good la tahayoo;
Mid baad garab laxaadliyo
Ruux guda abaaloo,
Loo galo wanaag iyo
Gaashaan la tahayoo;

Garaadlaay xogtaadii
Cidi gaadhi waydee
Dadkan kugu gabaabsiyey
Kumaa helay guntaadoo
Gacan-qaad la siiyaa?
Miyey gabi habaabeen?

Did you tear up all natal traits,
redraft infancy and all its rites?
Or did truth grow old, and find
its essence not eternal after all?
Where does the failure lie?

Your usual impact is to put
the people in two minds,
to keep them from deciding:
one casts you as the hero
they could never see back down;
while another thinks you short of wits –
your way lost, your well dry –
a barren camel; another one
misses you as he'd miss his own son –
if a speck of grit scratched you
he could not be consoled;
one casts you as cobra,
trustless as a looter; while another
has you as the strong shoulder,
a sure repayer of kindness,
deserving of good deeds,
a shelter and a shield.

Unquantified soul, secret from yourself,
ungraspable for others –
they all fall short in the fathoming.
Did anyone ever track you down
and shake you by the hand
or did they all end up lost?

Maadigaa wax gabayoo
Hadba geed is-mariyoo,
Goobba midab la joogoo
Gallibaxa habeenkii?

Garaad-daran naftaydaay!
In kastoon gucleeyoo,
Garmaamada haldhaagiyo
Gammaankaba ka jiitoo
Cirka sare galaa-baxo,
Adigay la gooshoo

Iga gaabinaynoo,
Goobtaan is-taagaba
Adigaa galluubane,
Ma gashaygu baaqdoo
Lagu yidhi ka soo goo?
Mise gaari inan oo
Guur-u-meer ah baad tahay?
Maxaad gama' u diiddee
Iga daba-gureysaa?

Dambiyaal waxaan galo
Ama geysto fool-xumo,
Gabigoodba ceebaha
Aan gaar u leeyahay,
In kastoon is-giijoo
Weji kale gashada oo
Dadka been ku gaasiro,
Adigaa giraanoo

Or could it be you who fails them?
Hiding within your shapeshifting,
a different colour for each place,
each night a new beast, a different face?

I can't get to grips with this garrulous self
even if my lope outstrips
the galloping of ostriches or horses,
even if I vanish from their horizons,
enter and depart from orbit
in the same instant you are with me,

you never fall short of my side.
Wherever I stand, whenever I stop,
you stand and stop with me
as though I carried round a debt
and someone said, 'Collect it!'
as though you were a good catch,
a woman looking for a husband.
Why is it you never sleep,
following me everywhere?

Whatever crime I commit,
whatever ugliness I enter into;
each shameful deed
that is my very own –
even though I gird myself to lie,
pull on another mask
to leave people at a loss –
you record each defect

Gunta iimahaygoo,
Hoos ii guhaadshee;
Godobtiyo xumaantada
Inaad tahay ninkeed-gaba,
Maxaad iigu garataa?

Garaad-daran naftaydaay!
Gumaysaad ku nooshoo
Dadkaa kugu garaacdoo,
Guddoonkooda mooyee
Kaa gareysan maayaan
Waxad adigu goysee;

Maad galabsan hawlaha
Kugu gaardiyaayee,
Galbiskii adoogaa
Goco oo ilmeeyoo,

Hooyadaa u goohoo
Galabtay ku dihatiyo
Eerso uur-galkaagii.

as though set down on tape,
insidiously fill me with guilt,
obligation, injury:
you see through me as a wife does –
but why understand me by my flaws?

Curious, gregarious, garrulous self,
did you fail to grasp the stifling norms?
To quarrel with those who rap our knuckles
for whom only their diktats
need be acknowledged,
and not what you conclude:

You don't deserve the problems
that barrack and assail you.
Remember the marriage ceremony
of your father and weep;

bewail your mother because of
the afternoon you entered her womb
and the world, blame her.

Uurkubbaale

'Cawdu billoo balooy baydh.'
'Bismillaahi "Yaasiin".'
Botorkiyo ciyaartoo
Sidaa lagu bilaaboo,
Anna biito-biitiyo
Bille-jire ku dheelaan
Beri hore garaadsaday.

Dadka waxan ka bawsaday:
'Dhool bari ka hirey baa
Dhaanka loo bariiyaa'.
Gabaygana Burhaanoow
Waxa aniga lay baray
Inu laba u kala baxo
Beeshana u kala yahay:

Waxay Biliso igu tidhi:
'Hadday maanso beer tahay
Run baa lagu biyeeyaa.
Bilicsiga dareenkaa
Lagu baalaleeyaa;
Xaq baa lagu bac-rimiyaa.
Baaqbaaqa noloshiyo
Biyo-dhiijinteediyo
Xilligay ku biqishaa.

Seer

In my cradle I heard the women sing
'In the name of God, "Yaasin"':
this is how we begin,
with the dance step and the dance.
I was playing 'biito biiti',
singing 'Bille-jire' –
this is how Gaarriye grew.

I suckled on hearsay, drank in lore:
'A cloud in the east means rest your feet,
the rain will trek to us.'
Dear friend, dear Burhaan, I was taught
there are two types of poem:
that which tells you how things are
and that with another agenda –
the people know which is which.

When she brought me up, Biliso said,
'If a poem is a farm
then how things truly are, that's water;
the best words for the best thoughts,
that's how it begins.
Justice is your only compost,
life itself is what you hoe:
just squeeze truth from what happens
and in its own time it will sprout.

'Midho waxay u bixisaa
Habka loo barbaarshiyo
Barta lagu abqaalaa.
Sida loogu baahdaa
Loo buushe-bixiyaa;
Ama loo bislaystaa.'

'Waxa lagu bardaanshaa
Baqoolka iyo geeddiga
Fac kastaa intuu bogo.
Bullashada dagaalkana
Bunduqay tilmaantaa.'

'Waa buun wax lagu hago;
Boodaanta yeedhmada
Bigil ereygu leeyahay.
Caws baar leh weeyaan;
Lana baxay sabool-diid
Soddon laguma baayaco.
Boqor laguma caabudo.
Biidhi-qaatennimo iyo
Baqas waa ka xaaraan.'

'Waana biime liidda ah,
Boqnihiisa lama xidho.
Nin baqdaa ma halabsado;
Bayd-gaabku kuma galo;
Beentana wax kuma laha.
Waa Bilan ma-geyno ah;
Bog-dooxeedu waa sino.'

'Whether a poem brings forth seeds
depends on how it's tended and by whom –
the spot in which it's planted;
depending on who needs it and for what
its husk is hulled or boiled.'

'A poem is the measure for
that trek beneath the draining sun
each generation adds to;
when you have to stand and fight
it shows you where to point the gun.'

'It guides you like a conch shell horn,
the call of the large camel bell;
it is the words' own bugle.
It is the finest matting, woven for a bride,
the one the song calls 'Refuser of poor suitors'.
It's not sold for coppers,
it's not for praising the powerful;
to put a price on it, any price,
cheapens it and is forbidden.'

'It's riding bareback on an unbroken horse –
you don't hobble its heels.
Those who fear for their hides
and won't ride without a saddle,
those lacking in the craft, can't get near this:
lies have nothing to do with it.
Poetry is a woman you do not betray,
to abuse her beauty is a sin.'

* * *

'Waxay bilic wax dheer tahay;
Iyadoon bariidada
Ballankeedi ka hor dhicin,
Kolkay bocorta maansado,
Adoo baalku kaa qoyey
Xadantana u baahnaa,
Sidii baalalleey iyo
Balanbaallis qalimo leh,
Ooy ubax baraarugay
Isku waa-bariisteen.'

'Bogga kuu salaaxdee
Burcad kuugu duugtee,
Bu'da leebka kugu mudan
Baydari-abbaartee,
Bulxankeedu laba-dhaca
Sida uur-ku-baalaha,
Boogahaaga hoosiyo
Bayrtaada qoomee.'

'Kolba baaq xiloodin ah
Barta aad u nogoshahay
Intuu baac u sii dego,
Tixda miino-baadhkii
Fiix kugu biskootiyo
Dhul bacdii ku taal iyo,

* * *

'It's most lovely when most perfectly timed,
as though, met at morning,
you exchanged greetings
at just the right moment.
When your own wings feel so bedraggled
that you need another's touch,
then the full beauty of a poem
is like a butterfly meeting
a just-wakened flower
at the exact moment of dawn.'

'When it seems to caress your flank,
to massage a salve into you;
when the pupil of its arrow pierces you
striking the mark exactly,
splitting your anguished cries in two.
Like a seer who peers inside you,
it homes in on your over-sensitivities,
your innermost wounds.'

'When you suddenly hear of your betrothal
it sends the message deeper
into your most vulnerable point.
Poetry is the mine-seeker
opening your old, scarred-over hurt,
discovering your untouched earth,

Ku banayso meel aan
Beryahaaba gacal dayin.'

'Ee baahi-laawuhu
Adigoo basiiro leh
Intuu boodhka kaa tumo,
Xiisaha basaasiyo
Beer-qaado laabtee,
Tuduc wali gun iyo baar
Meel baas ku taabtee,
Intuu baaxad le'eg yahay
Isagoo banbaane ah
Badhtankaaga ka sanqadho.'

'Ee kugu ballaadhee
Markii bayd la sheegaba,
Sidii baal qarsoodi ah
La bac dhabay xogtaadii,
Hadba baallo-daymada
Faraq-bood ka qaaddee.'

Maansada ba'leeyda ah
Ee baadi-soocda leh,
Bog kastoo la soo rogo
Sir aad bixisay mooddee,
Nafta oo baraad li'i:
Kolba 'baga!' tidhaahdiyo,
'Bishmaha Eebbe kuma jaro.
Ninka yidhi run badanaa!
Ma afkaygu kala baxay?'

that place closed off
from those closest to you.'

'When Baahi-laawe, that dancing verse,
brushes the melancholy from you
as though it were a dust
that settled on your lust for life,
choked the desire in your chest;
it's like a grenade, a bomb,
its blast-range perfectly judged
so each stanza touches you
from problematic top to troubled toe,
exploding from your core.'

'When it permeates you
each time a line is recited
as though from a secret page
on which your own secrets are exposed
so that each time you scan it
you jolt with anxiety.'

This poem alliterates in 'b'
but all the best poems are branded
so that each page which is turned
makes you believe you've confessed
and each time your soul
involuntarily cries out, 'Bravo!
Dear God, don't seal this man's lips –
may the truth he speaks continue
as though it burst from my own mouth.'

Geeridii Ina Boqor

'Xaye cala salaa'
'Xaye calal falaax'
Xilli loo addimay
Ma xusuusan karo;
Xilna waa jiraa
Waana xaal-adduun;
Xiddigihi cirkana
Xalaa laygu yidhi:
"Xinjireey liqeen".

Dhulku wuu xarkagay
Sidii xuuko geel
Waanu xiiran yahay.
Xooluhu dhammaan
Waa xaaluf-daaq.

Xaggu waa qaniin
Xaggu lama-degaan;
Xidhku waa saliid,
Daad-xoor dab-liyo
Xadhig-lama-sitaan
Ku dul xeeran yiin.

Xaggu waa bacaad
Xanfar iyo dabayl;
Malaa waa xagaa.

Death of a Princess

Xaye cala salaa
Come to prayer
Xaye cala falaax
Come to salvation
I can't remember
which prayer time it was
but I had to answer.
It may be the way of this world
beneath the witness of the stars
but last night I was told,
'They gorged on clotted blood.'

The earth there is dry and gleaming
scraped smooth
like camel fat.
All the goats and sheep
have grazed the land bare.

The place is ridden with ticks,
a desert where no-one can rest,
a scrubland sitting on oil;
floods of people with guns
and without restraints
surround it.

The place is duned,
with a humid wind;
it is, perhaps, the hottest time.

Xaggu waa masniyo
Fooq iyo xaraar
Isha xiijiyoo;
Demesh iyo xariir
Ku xiddaysanoo
Cirka soo xansada.
Oo dad loo xil-qabo
Xamastoodu taal.

Togag baa dhex xula;
Biyii Xaramka iyo
Wiski xooriyaa
Dhex xumbaynayaan.

Xaggu waa dar-xumo;
Xaawaleey carruur
Ku xansheeran oo,
Xiiq iyo harraad
Xuurteeysan iyo
Xammaal iyo wastaad.

Afartaasi xidhan.

Xaggan kalena eeg:
Gabadheenna Xiis
Waa xabag-barsheed;
Waa xero-u-dhalan
Xulad geenyo ugub.
Oon xiito guluf
Dirir iyo xabbaadh
Loo sudhin xakame.

It is also cities
sprouting skyscrapers
which exhaust the eye,
furnished and fringed
with damask and silk;
they eavesdrop on air's gossip.
This is where those responsible
hoard their possessions.

Rivers flow within that land,
waters of the Holy Places
and whisky foam
and froth up there.

The place is misery itself,
women burdened with children
hawking and gasping,
bearers and bricklayers
ground down and harassed.

My first quarter is done.
Look still more closely:
see our young woman, Xiis,
wholesome as a honeycomb,
born within the pale.
Like the choicest virgin mare,
she isn't bridled for
some camel raid, nor
a share of the loot.

Waa xuural-cayn;
Iyo Xaaliyeey
Dayax xoosh ahoo
Xalay gaadh ahaa,
Saakana xarrago
Xil-wareejintii,
Xuubkii cirkiyo
Daahyadi xidhnaa
Kor u xaydayoo;

Sagal xaradhyo lihi
Qorrax xiiso wado,
Xaraaraha bulka leh
Ku xiddeeyeyoo;

Xod-xodtooy iyana
Xaradhaamadiyo
Hab-xiloodintii
Xadantootayoo;

Xummad iyo kulayl
Naf-xaraare baas,
Xaam-xaamadkii
Xayn furatay oo
Xusul joogga le'eg.
Xaashaa kallaa!
Xubno-jeedalleey
Haddii aan xistiyey
"Xaal qaado" dhaha.

She is Heaven's eye, a houri;
she is the sun, sharing
the horizon with the moon
who last night guarded the earth
and this morning passes on
his watch, elegantly
drawing back the hem,
the membrane of the sky
like closed curtains.

He paints the dawn sky
as she rises in her urgency
with the fletches on the arrows
of the morning's rays.

And she, in this flirtation,
because of his caresses,
these delicate advances,
lets herself be roused.

In her fever and her heat,
her rising and ripping,
self-consuming passion,
she throws off her clouds
and stands, the length of a forearm
from the horizon. Can you see
her whip-lithe limbs?
If I've failed
then ask her to forgive me.

* * *

Gabadheenna Xiis
Xubin bay ahayd
Xuddun webi ku taal;
Oo xidh oodan iyo
Xakab loo dugsiyo;
Oon xagaaga arag
Dhirta xaalufshiyo
Xanaf iyo kulayl.

Mar uun bay 'xaf' tidhi;
Mar uun bay Xorriyo
Ka kufriday xumii;
Laye Xaawo hee!
Xadhka-gooysayaa;
Xadki jabisayaa.

Is-xabaal wax badan
Godka uu xabkiyo
Xinjiraha ku cuno,
Huwin jirey xariir
Ka xayuubisaa;
Xin u qaawisaa;
Ceebaha xilka leh
Xabbad-qaaddayaa.

Geedkii xaskiyo
Xuladada wax guba
Xaabuu u yahay
Loogu xeeban jirey,

* * *

Dearly-missed, our Xiis
was a navel to the river
of the people; she was part of them,
but penned in scrubland,
and fenced in the pen,
she did not have to see
that season which sears the trees,
feel its harshness or its heat.

Only once did she break out
only once feel the freedom
of transgressing their strictures.
It was said of Eve that she
cut the rope that bound her,
breached her limits.

And so she tore the silk off
that used to cover the hole
in which the rat eats
afterbirth and blood clots,
deliberately exposing
its shameful weaknesses,
its irresponsibilities:
she set them out one by one.

That tree, the twigs
and dry branches of which were kindling,
the dead leaves a fuel
which used to threaten fire,

Inu xabag-dhunkaal
Xordan yahay dadkii
U xaqiijisaa.

Xubbi iyo kalgacal
Laab xuunsho galay
La xariidisaa;
Dareenkeeda xalan
Iyadoon xidh-xidhin,
Hanadkii xasladay
Xiiseeysayaa;
Xasil diiddayaa.

Xusbaddana ma gelin
Inay xilo nin tahay
Qasab loogu xidhay;
Xaaleeyna-mayn
Xaafaddeey ka timi,
Iyo Xaaliyeey
Xeerkii ka jirey.

* * *

Waxay xawlisaba
Xanti durugtayaa;
Xogsigii horeba
Xigtadii Gobaad,
Dir-xumaan-ku-nool
Ka xanaaqdayaa;
Baha-xaydho-weyn
Xayraantayaa.

she confirmed to the people
as hollow, a tree
of poisonous resin.

She disclosed our strongest feelings,
that intense intimacy of love,
which enters into us all;
she longed for her elegant boy
who swept her away;
by not closing off
her clean desires,
she refused stability.

She didn't consider how,
betrothed through obligation,
she was another man's wife;
nor took into account
that place she came from,
nor, poor girl,
the law that holds sway there.

* * *

As this liaison continued
it went beyond whispers.
As soon as the secret was out
the family of that princess,
those wrong-doers,
grew wrathful;
that gluttonous House
got angry.

Gabadhii Xaddiyo
Caashaqa ku xidhay
'Laan-gaabka xune
Xagga sare ahayn,
Xulashada gurracan
Ee sumal-xadka ah'
Ku xujoowdayaa;
Xabsi loo diryaa.

Iyadoon Xorriyo
Aan cidi xukumin
Qalbigii xallaa,
Xaramkii cishqiga
Xadradoow ahaa,
Taalladi xubbiga
Xabbad lagu furyaa.

Laye Xaadsan iyo
Xuurkeey jeclayd
Loogu xiiryeyaa;
La xabaalyeyaa.

Halna waa xusuus
Sheekada ku xidho:
Meeshu waa Xijaas
Xaruntii waxyiga
Halka loo xaj tago,
Ee Xabiibalaah
Xudduntiisu tahay.

That gifted girl
was found guilty of what?
Love that was tethered to
'the branch with short roots
that can't reach the heights;
the wild choice
of the wrong ram' –
so they threw her in jail.

Then, although no-one tried her,
that Holy Place of love
which was a seat for
her clean heart,
that shrine to passion
was opened by a bullet.

This is how it was told:
she and the boy she loved
were cut down
and put in their graves.

If you only remember one thing
about this story, let it be this:
the place is Hijaz,
the centre of the divine revelation,
destination of the hajj;
it is the navel of the Prophet,
where the Beloved of God was born.

Aadmi

Aadmiyahaw hallaysani!
Ambadyahaw wareersani!
Maqal ereyadaydoo!

Buuraha ag joogsoo
Amakaag daraaddii,
Ilmo gabax ka siiyoo!

Cirka sare u eegoo
Xiddiggaha astaysoo
Arag felegga meeroo!

Onkodkiyo hillaaciyo
Ufadaa dhacaysiyo
Uurada waraysoo.

Ololkeeda Gooraan
Aammus oo dhegeysoo
Shimbiraha la ooyoo.

Badda 'aw'-da haysiyo
Waxa uurka ugu jira
Axadhoo garwaaqsoo.

Dhulka aad u baadhoo,
Webiyada ordaayiyo
Daruuraha indheeyoo.

Arrogance

Wandered brood of Adam,
lost, bewildered people,
hear what I have to say.

Stop for a moment before the mountains
and for the simple sake of awe
be humbled, let your tears fall.

Look to, look through the air above,
be moved by the sight of stars,
watch their bodies wheel.

Ask the thunder, see what lightning says,
the rain-bearing wind which blows
the good grey cloud, ask them.

The camel's old keen for her calf,
be hushed and hear it, hear how
the birds' song weeps with it: weep with them too.

How the sea sounds out its old chorus,
what moves in its abyssal womb:
acknowledge these and what they mean.

Examine the earth at your feet,
the rush of the rivers,
raise your eyes to the clouds.

Oogada jalleecoo
Ciirada aroortiyo
Dabaylaha af gara oo.

Uduggooda kaymaha
Urso oo jeclaysoo
Ku ilwaadso dooggoo.

U abtiri naflaydoo
Ayaamaha tilmaansoo
Aabiga bilaashka ah,
Waa inaad illowdaa!

Afaggaalayaashiyo
Cadceeddeenna oloshiyo
Awrka samada yaa yidhi,
Aadmigay u shidanyiin?

Ifkoon cidi ku uunnayn,
Miyaan Dirirku oognayn?
Ururradu miyaanay
Kaa ayni weynayn?
Ilayskooda goormaa
Loo daaray awgaa?

Hadmaa felegga oosha ah
Amar buuxa lagu yidhi
Ku ekaw dadkoo qudha?
 Haddaad eegga madhataan,

Glimpse what lies above
the auroral mist, the winds,
understand what these things have to say.

The scent of wild acacia –
inhale it, relish it, and
delight in the green of pastures.

Count up the lineage of all life,
mark the endless days and days:
this worthless arrogance of yours,
you have to let it go.

All nebulae and galaxies,
the Camel of the Southern Cross,
our own burning sun, who said these
were lit for humankind?

Before a man was made in this world
didn't Virgo blaze above?
Aren't all those gatherings of stars
far older than us?
Since when was their high light
kindled only for you?

Exactly when do you think the heavens
were told to carry out the order
'Confine yourselves to the human race'?
If you simply ceased to be

Miyaanuu iftiimayn,
Sidiisaa ahaanayn?

Aadmiyahaw hallaysani!
Amarkaagu waa been!
Waxaad uur wadaagtaan
Ugaadhaa wareegtoo
Ugbaadkiyo caleentaad
Uur wada gasheenoo.

Uumiyaha dhammaantii
Ilma-adeer gudboon iyo
Isir baad tihiinoo;
Noolahaad arkaysaa
Waa ul iyo diirkeed;
Waa sida indhaha oo
Kolkay midi ilmaysaa
Ta kaleeto ooydaa;
Looma uumin keligaa
Inay kuu adeegaan.

Ammuuraha badh baa sir ah;
Sida xaal u eg yahay
Ujeeddadu ka xeeldheer.

wouldn't their light continue?
Wouldn't it be then as it is now?

Wandered brood of Adam,
your bluster is a lie.
You shared this womb with all
wild things that roam,
all roots that flourish,
you entered this world together.

All creation is your cousin,
each creature your equal
and you share an ancestor:
all living things are to you
as stick is to bark, bark to stick.
You and they are like two eyes –
when one sheds tears
the other weeps.
They were not made for you alone,
nor were they created to serve.

Of everything which is, half is secret –
however things appear
the meaning is always deeper.

Wootargayt

Wiswis bayga galay Kaartarow weheshigiinniiye
Waayo-arag wixii aan ka helay buugaggii weriyey
Wareerkaad baddeen buu khalqigu weli la taahaaye.
Su'aalaan ku weyddiinayaa ila sal waaweyne;
Walaalnimadii aan koolin jirey waadhka yaa geliyey?
Nabaddiyo wanaaggii ayaa wegeredkow gooyey
Isagoo takoor wada ayaa laba-wejiileeyey?
Waadaasha xoolaha lumaa weere waw halise
Wedkii Maalkam Eges waan ka naxay wacad Ilaaheeye.
Hadba weerka naag baw xidhaan weydey kii qabaye
Kolka geesi weyraxo ayaa dacar waraabsiiya?
Yaa wadey raggii Luudar Kiin waagi hanaq-gooyey?
Hindidii casayd yaa waddarey wadarna yaw laayey?
Alle weger waxaa belo dhigteen waa ka waasacane!
Niksan wayla sahal ceeb haddaad ka werweraysaane,
Qirta Wootargaytyadu ka badan taydin weriseene!

Walbahaarka Falastiin nin ogi qulub la weydoowye
Waa debed-wareeggii sidii 'woohow' loo yidhiye
Waddankoodi goortii la dhacay wahabku kooreeye.
Waagii kastaba Pii El Oo waw dagaal wicide
Ummaddaasi wadhan yaa sidaa waajib kaga yiilay?
Miyaan lala wadaagayn Yuhuud wiirsigiyo ceebta?
Alle weger waxaa belo dhigteen waa ka waasacane!
Niksan wayla sahal ceeb haddaad ka werweraysaane,
Qirta Wootargaytyadu ka badan taydin weriseene!

Watergate

Carter, I grow cautious of your camaraderie,
As I've come to understand, from what I've read, I'm wary:
Humanity cries out still at the confusion that you've caused.
There are questions I want answered, and, to my mind, they are crucial:
That comradeship I once acclaimed, who put it in a corner?
Who cut the camel's girth-strap that secured both peace and virtue?
Who was two-faced here, very like a segregator?
What's parted from the flock becomes hyena quarry.
The cutting down of Malcolm X, God knows, that hurt me to the quick,
As does each time a widow has to wear the keening scarf.
The hero's wrath, who is it that has watered it with aloe?
Who was it led the cut-throats straight to Martin Luther King?
Who massacred Red Indians, and slaughtered them in multitudes?
As God is my witness you've wasted a vastness.
If you cared about shame, then Nixon was the least of it.
Confess: there are more Watergates than you admit.

To know the pains of Palestine should make you wane with woe,
They wander through all nations like a host of scatterlings.
While their land is plundered, they are saddled with despair,
Each dawn the PLO is wakened up to war.
Who forced its hand in this and cast that nation out to drift?
Who's guarantor to guile and shares in Israel's disgrace?
As God is my witness you've wasted a vastness.
If you cared about shame, then Nixon was the least of it.
Confess: there are more Watergates than you admit.

Fiyatnaam wixii aad baddeen uunku wada yaabye
Sida dhibic wajiineed wixii gumuc is-weydaartey
Nin waraystay waa garanayaa wahanki Saygoone.
Miinawaarro dhagaraysanoo cudur walwaalaaya
Iyo nacab dayuurado wataa geliyey weesaaqe
Raggaad waranka siiseen anoo weli u ooyaaya
Marna waxaan i deynayn duqii ugu fil-weynaaye
Waheey geeridii Hoo Shi Miin wiilashay gudhaye.
Alle weger waxaa belo dhigteen waa ka waasacane!
Niksan wayla sahal ceeb haddaad ka werweraysaane,
Qirta Wootargaytyadu ka badan taydin weriseene!

Woobiga Angoolee qarxaday wiririgtii yeedhay
Boortuqiiski wiiqay rabeen inay ku waabshaane
Goortuu wadnaha taabtay bay wegen u fuuleene.
Waxay waarrisaba maalintay calanki waaheeshay
Waqalkiyo daruurihi onkoday webiyadii dooxmay;
Guushii markii loo walqalay Neeto wirif-raadshey
In wakiil u tago Yuu En Oo golaha waageeran
Maan garan halkuu weyd ka yahay waajibkaa cadiye,
Wadhiyeey maxaad ugu riddeen welegta viitowga?
Alle weger waxaa belo dhigteen waa ka waasacane!
Niksan wayla sahal ceeb haddaad ka werweraysaane,
Qirta Wootargaytyadu ka badan taydin weriseene!

Your mayhem made in Vietnam has left the world appalled
Where bullets, switching billets, drop like cold rain in the night,
And anyone who seeks out news grasps Saigon is in agony:
Trustless man-o'-wars carry cargoes there of plague,
And bombers are the people's foe for bringing down miasma–
I weep here for the sake of those that you put to the spear.
The memory of their elder, that great statesman, never leaves me
Until my eyes run dry of tears for the loss of Ho Chi Minh –
As God is my witness you've wasted a vastness.
If you cared about shame, then Nixon was the least of it.
Confess: there are more Watergates than you admit.

In Angola war explodes, until the clash of combat deafens
Where they'd halt the Portuguese, who made the people poor:
When their hearts were quickened, and they mounted steeds to fight,
The struggle then continued till their banners flew on high.
When the rain clouds clapped, and the rivers broke their banks,
And as that win won loud acclaim, still Neto would not hush:
An ambassador must go to where the UN held assembly.
Who could follow how this failed when what was needful was so
    clear?
Why would you choose to wield then that dishonourable veto?
As God is my witness you've wasted a vastness.
If you cared about shame, then Nixon was the least of it.
Confess: there are more Watergates than you admit.

Sida ceel wiyiiraad kol hore nooga wabaxdeene
Warshaddiinna dhiiggaan tufaa lagu waraabshaaye;
Garaad ma laha ruuxii wabiin wacad la qaataaye
Ka il-baxay wallaahida afka ah walalac beenaade.
Werwerkii Simbaabwaan qabaa Weris-la-mooddiiye
Waadiga Namiibiya rag baa waayir xidhayaaye
Idinkaa watee Yaan Ismiidh wadhaf ma tuureene.
Alle weger waxaa belo dhigteen waa ka waasacane!
Niksan wayla sahal ceeb haddaad ka werweraysaane,
Qirta Wootargaytyadu ka badan taydin weriseene!

You've already drunk your fill from us as from a salty well.
Your workshops are all watered by the precious blood I spit.
Siding with a conman leaves us comprehending nothing –
At length I learned to tell the tone of oaths from sparkling lies.
Then I worried with Zimbabwe that was beautiful as Weris
That in Namibia's wadi men are cordoned in with wire.
And this is down to you, or Smith would not have slung a stone–
As God is my witness you've wasted a vastness.
If you cared about shame, then Nixon was the least of it.
Confess: there are more Watergates than you admit.

Afterword

I am watching TV on a hot summer's evening. The President of the United States is leading a crowd in North Carolina as they chant: 'Send her back, send her back.' Their target is a young Somali Congresswoman, Ilhan Omar. For many in the Somali diaspora, such racism is an everyday fact. But Omar responds, as so many Somalis do, with a refusal to step down from political life. With absolute grace. And with poetry. Quoting Maya Angelou she tweets:

> You may shoot me with your words,
> You may cut me with your eyes,
> You may kill me with your hatefulness,
> But still, like air, I'll rise.

Soon #IStandWithIlhanOmar is trending on Twitter around the globe.

Poetry and politics are deeply entwined in Somali culture. It is poets who speak truth to power. This collection contains a new translation of Gaarriye's poem 'Watergate' ('Wootargayt') in which he rails against America and the Americanisation of the world: a state of sordid racism, in which the primal scene of violence, the slaughter of Native Americans, seems to ripple out, touching Palestine, Vietnam, Africa. 'If you cared about shame, then Nixon was the least of it', Gaarriye writes, as if in awful premonition. 'As God is my witness you've wasted a vastness'. And we are all still wasting that vastness – the vastness of love, of nature, of human potential, of holiness. Still, in our smallness and meanness, we elect such small, mean men.

Gaarriye was, to all who knew him, the opposite of small and mean – charismatic, generous, expansive, confident in the knowledge that Somali poetry is one of the world's great poetries. When I first began co-translating the UK-Somali poet Asha Lul Mohamud Yusuf with Said Jama Hussein and Maxamed Xasan 'Alto' years ago, I quickly realised both how technically astonishing Somali poetry is and how central it is to the community. Soon I was a regular at Somali Week each autumn in Bethnal Green, organised by Kayd, attending poetry events at which rapturous audiences chanted along with every word. Afterwards, talking to these poetry fans, I would always hear the same name: Gaarriye. You must hear Gaarriye! Gaarriye is the great poet!

Maxamed Xaashi Dhamac 'Gaarriye' (1949-2012) was one of the most important figures in 20th century Somali literature. He was the initiator of the famous 'Deelley', a chain of poems by Somali poets in 1979-80 that spoke powerfully to the politics of the time and is still being added to now by poets such as Asha Lul. Watch Gaarriye on YouTube videos and, even without understanding the language, you get some sense of his charm. Unlike many of our 'significant' male poets, he does not disport himself like a 'major' figure or silver-back gorilla, constantly namedropping or trying to underline his own seriousness. Gaarriye is animated, funny, gesturing with his hands, laughing with the audience, connecting with them. And you can hear too the impeccable craft – the alliteration (traditional Somali poems alliterate on a single letter); the perfect metre. This is high art that is for everyone – the 'best words for the best thoughts' as his poem 'Uurkubbaale' ('Seer') has it. Rich, human, tragicomic, his vision fits the self-portrait he creates in the wonderful 'Garaad-Daran' ('Self-Misunderstood'), which alliterates in G – the poet as garrulous, self-confessedly guilty, gregarious, ungraspable.

Through the Poetry Translation Centre's founder, Sarah Maguire (who was always first up during the dancing at Somali

Week), I soon met Gaarriye's translators Martin Orwin and Bill Herbert. They are the perfect pairing of talents: Martin's deep knowledge and respect for Somali culture is visible in every line of these translations, whereas Bill brings a sort of genius very similar to Gaarriye's own: his own writing is witty, mercurial, layered, able to make an audience giggle then switch to gravitas.

Looking at a poem like 'Aadmi' ('Arrogance') in Martin and Bill's stunning translation, you can see how Gaarriye managed to both respect Somali traditions and freshen them up, taking them somewhere new. In a trope that relates to the fact they are written for performance rather than the page, many Somali poems begin with a direct introductory address to the gathered audience, an *arar*, explaining why they have composed the poem and requesting that people listen. In 'Arrogance' it becomes an address to humanity itself, and their attention a kind of redemption:

> Wandered brood of Adam,
> lost, bewildered people,
> hear what I have to say.
>
> Stop for a moment before the mountains
> and for the simple sake of awe
> be humbled, let your tears fall.

The rhetorical device of asking questions, common in Somali political poems, is, similarly, elevated to a contemplation of the universe itself, in a poem of deep wisdom and humility:

> All nebulae and galaxies,
> the Camel of the Southern Cross,
> our own burning sun, who said these
> were lit for humankind?

The conclusion of such poems, the *gebaggebo* or ending, is often a kind of prayer or reminder to praise Allah, something Gaarriye echoes but with much greater subtly, drawing on a sense of the deep mystery of existence in his last lines:

> Of everything which is, half is secret –
> however things appear
> the meaning is always deeper.

'Geeridii Ina Boqor' ('Death of a Princess') – based on a well-known, controversial docu-drama by Antony Thomas of the same name about a Saudi princess executed for adultery – is a poem that shows off another of Gaarriye's strengths, his famous ability with metaphors. It creates a vivid, dystopian landscape, 'duned', tick-ridden, 'dry and gleaming / scraped smooth / like camel fat'. A young woman transgresses and in a memorable, heart-stopping passage we are told:

> In her fever and her heat,
> her rising and ripping,
> self-consuming passion,
> she throws off her clouds
> and stands, the length of a forearm
> from the horizon. Can you see
> her whip-lithe limbs?
> If I've failed
> then ask her to forgive me.

The speaker's intimate relationship with his audience is used to startling effect. As in the final verse where, after she and the boy she loves have been killed and buried, he addresses us directly again:

> If you only remember one thing
> about this story, let it be this:

> the place is Hijaz,
> the centre of the divine revelation,
> destination of the hajj

To remember only this is, on some level, to put the entire story we've just heard – a tawdry drama about human passion and murder; flirtation and gluttony; rats sniffing the afterbirth; honeycomb and poisonous resin – out of our minds. The whole poem is a sticky trap; unimportant as the 'air's gossip', which we must shun in favour of divine revelation. It is an audacious conclusion.

The new translation in this collection, 'Wootargayt' ('Watergate'), is a ferocious addition to Gaarriye's poems in English, and the masterclass in how to write an urgent, political poem that we need right now. Somali poets are often treated almost like politicians, and expected to use their platform to advocate for social change. This is a poem of righteous anger, sonically heightened (in this translation) by the almost contemptuous alliteration on the c of Carter. But there are also those human moments and astonishing images: the woman with her 'keening scarf'; bullets that 'drop like cold rain' on Vietnam. With the USA having tortured so many people around the world, the poem stages a kind of poetic role-reversal. White, male, authoritatian America, embodied in the figure of Carter, is tortured with the relentless list of his own crimes; urged to 'confess'. Although Watergate (and so many other -gates) are long passed, Trump's shamelessness in power means it still feels horrifically relevant.

Amongst Somali-speaking people, Gaarriye could not be more revered. Elsewhere, it is a great shame that Gaarriye's name is not held with the same esteem in the English-speaking world as other 20th century giants who moved between the political and the philosophical with similar ease, such as Heaney, Miłosz or Walcott. It speaks of a racist and colonial inattention to African literature, that means it has been untranslated and neglected. PTC founder Sarah Maguire's passionate enthusiasm did much to raise awareness of Somali poetry over the last decade, and this book will hopefully introduce more people to one of its masters. Sadly, since the project began both Gaarriye and Sarah have died, but their beloved poetry remains vividly alive in these pages. As 'Seer' tells us:

> the full beauty of a poem
> is like a butterfly meeting
> a just-wakened flower
> at the exact moment of dawn.

Clare Pollard

Maxamed Xaashi Dhamac 'Gaarriye' was born in Hargeysa, Somaliland. He is regarded as one of the most important Somali poets of the twentieth century, having composed groundbreaking poems on a wide range of contemporary and classical themes. In addition to his poems he made a significant contribution to the public understanding of Somali poetry forms, writing the first article on thi stopic for a national newspaper in 1976. He died in 2012.

W.N. Herbert was born in Dundee. He has published seven volumes of poetry and four pamphlets, and is widely anthologised. He has been shortlisted twice for the T.S. Eliot prize and twice for the Saltire. In 2013 he was appointed Dundee's Makar, or city laureate. In 2014 he was awarded a Cholmondeley Prize for his poetry, and in 2015 he became a Fellow of the Roayl Society of Literature.

Martin Orwin has taught at the School of Oriental and African Studies, London, since 1992 and is currently Senior Lecturer in Somali and Amharic. He has published many articles on Somali language and poetry, and has carried out research in the Horn of Africa. His translations of Somali poems have appeared in *Modern Poetry in Translation* and elsewhere.

Clare Pollard has published five collections of poetry, most recently *Incarnation* (Bloodaxe, 2017). Her co-translation with Said Jama Hussein and Maxamed Xasan 'Alto' of Asha Lul Mohamud Yusuf's *The Sea-Migrations* (Bloodaxe/PTC, 2017) was The Sunday Times Poetry Book of the Year. She edits *Modern Poetry in Translation*.

About the Poetry Translation Centre

Set up in 2004, the Poetry Translation Centre is the only UK organisation dedicated to translating, publishing and promoting contemporary poetry from Africa, Asia and Latin America. We introduce extraordinary poets from around the world to new audiences through books, online resources and bilingual events. We champion diversity and representation in the arts, and forge enduring relations with diaspora communities in the UK. We explore the craft of translation through our long-running programme of workshops which are open to all.

The Poetry Translation Centre is based in London and is an Arts Council National Portfolio organisation. To find out more about us, including how you can support our work, please visit:

www.poetrytranslation.org.

About the World Poet Series

The *World Poet Series* offers an introduction to some of the world's most exciting contemporary poets in an elegant pocket-sized format. The books are presented as bilingual editions, with the English and original-language text displayed side by side. The translations themselves have emerged from specially commissioned collaborations between leading English-language poets and translators. Completing each book is an afterword essay by a UK-based poet, responding to the translations.